Beloved Daughter: A 21-Day Devotional for Single Women in Their 30s

Nicole G M

INTRODUCTION

As a single woman in your 30s, life can be both exciting and challenging. You may be enjoying your independence and pursuing your passions, but you may also be navigating the pressures of society and the longing for a life partner. In the midst of all this, it can be easy to lose sight of your identity and purpose as a beloved child of God.

This devotional is written specifically for you, dear sister. It's a collection of 21 reflections designed to encourage you in your faith, strengthen you in your singleness, and remind you of God's unending love and grace. Each day's reading includes a passage of Scripture, a personal reflection, and a prayer.

Through this devotional, you will be invited to dive deeper into your relationship with God, embrace your unique calling and gifts, and find hope and joy in your season of singleness. You'll also be reminded that you are not alone, but are part of a community of single women who are also seeking to follow Christ and live purposeful lives.

Whether you are content in your singleness or struggling with it, this devotional is for you. It is a reminder that God sees you, loves you, and has a plan for your life that is greater than you could ever imagine. So let's begin this journey together, trusting in God's goodness and grace every step of the way.

Day 1: Finding Contentment in Singleness

I am not saying this because I am in need, for I have learned to be content whatever the circumstances. - Philippians 4:11

As a single woman in your 30s, it's easy to feel like something is missing in your life. You may have thought that you would have found your life partner by now, but for one reason or another, you find yourself still waiting. This can be a difficult and lonely season, but it can also be a time of growth and discovery.

In Philippians 4:11-13, the apostle Paul talks about finding contentment in all circumstances, whether in plenty or in need. He had learned to be content in every situation through Christ, who gave him strength. As a single woman, it can be easy to fall into the trap of thinking

THAT YOUR LIFE WILL ONLY BE COMPLETE WHEN YOU FIND A PARTNER. BUT TRUE CONTENTMENT AND FULFILLMENT CAN ONLY BE FOUND IN CHRIST.

TAKE SOME TIME TODAY TO REFLECT ON YOUR LIFE AND THE BLESSINGS THAT YOU HAVE. THINK ABOUT THE WAYS IN WHICH GOD HAS SHOWN HIS LOVE AND PROVISION FOR YOU. INSTEAD OF FOCUSING ON WHAT YOU DON'T HAVE, FOCUS ON WHAT YOU DO HAVE AND BE GRATEFUL FOR IT. ASK GOD TO HELP YOU FIND CONTENTMENT IN YOUR CURRENT SEASON AND TO TRUST IN HIS TIMING FOR YOUR LIFE.

PRAYER

DEAR GOD, THANK YOU FOR ALL THE BLESSINGS IN MY LIFE. HELP ME TO FIND CONTENTMENT IN MY CURRENT SEASON AND TO TRUST IN YOUR PLAN FOR MY FUTURE. GIVE ME STRENGTH AND PEACE AS I NAVIGATE THE UPS AND DOWNS OF LIFE AS A SINGLE WOMAN. IN JESUS' NAME, AMEN.

Day 2: Trusting in God's Timing

"For everything there is a season, a time for every activity under heaven." - Ecclesiastes 3:1

Being single at 30 can easily make you feel like time is running out. You may feel pressure from society, family, and even yourself to find a partner, settle down, and start a family. However, God's timing is perfect, and He has a plan for your life that is greater than your own desires and expectations.

It's important to remember that God's timing is not our own, and sometimes we may have to wait longer than we expected for certain things to happen in our lives. But in those times of waiting, we can trust that God is working behind the scenes, preparing us for what's to come and shaping us into the women He wants us to

BE.

We can also find comfort in the fact that we are not alone in our waiting. Many women throughout history have waited for God's timing, including Sarah, who waited decades for a child, and Ruth, who waited for a husband. Yet in both cases, God's timing was perfect, and He blessed them beyond what they could have imagined.

Prayer

Heavenly Father, help me to trust in Your timing, even when it doesn't match up with my own. Give me patience and peace as I wait for Your plan to unfold in my life. Help me to focus on Your promises and to remember that You are always with me. In Jesus' name, amen.

Day 3: Embracing Your Identity in Christ

"Therefore, if anyone is in Christ, the new creation has come: The old has gone, the new is here!" 2 Corinthians 5:17

Do you feel like your relationship status defines you? Society may try to convince you that you are incomplete or less than others because you're not married. However, as a believer in Christ, your identity is not found in your marital status but in your relationship with Him.

When you put your faith in Jesus, you become a new creation. The old you with all its flaws and shortcomings is gone, and a new you has emerged. You are no longer defined by your past, your mistakes, or your single status. You are a beloved child of God with a purpose and a destiny.

Embracing your identity in Christ means recognizing that you are valuable and loved, regardless of your relationship status. You are chosen, accepted, and equipped to live a fulfilling life. Your singleness is not a curse, but an opportunity to grow closer to God, pursue your passions and make a positive impact in the world. By embracing your identity in Christ, you can live with confidence, purpose, and joy, knowing that your worth comes from who you are in Him.

Prayer

Dear God, thank you for making me a new creation in Christ. Help me to embrace my identity in Him and not be defined by my relationship status. I pray that you would fill me with a sense of purpose and value and that you would use me to make a positive impact in the world. Help me to trust in your plan for my life

AND TO LIVE WITH JOY AND CONFIDENCE IN WHO I AM IN YOU. AMEN.

Day 4: Overcoming Fear and Anxiety

"So do not fear, for I am with you; do not be dismayed, for I am your God. I will strengthen you and help you; I will uphold you with my righteous right hand." - Isaiah 41:10

Fear and anxiety are common struggles that many of us face, especially in today's world where there is so much uncertainty and change happening all around us. But as a single woman in her 30s, you may also face unique fears and anxieties such as the fear of being alone or not finding a partner, the fear of missing out on experiences, or the anxiety of feeling like you're behind in life compared to your friends.

However, as a believer in Christ, you are called to trust in God's promises and not give in to fear and anxiety. Isaiah 41:10

REMINDS US THAT WE DO NOT NEED TO FEAR BECAUSE GOD IS WITH US. HE PROMISES TO STRENGTHEN US, HELP US, AND UPHOLD US WITH HIS RIGHTEOUS RIGHT HAND.

INSTEAD OF FOCUSING ON OUR FEARS AND ANXIETIES, WE CAN CHOOSE TO FOCUS ON GOD'S GOODNESS AND FAITHFULNESS. WE CAN ALSO TAKE PRACTICAL STEPS TO OVERCOME OUR FEARS AND ANXIETIES, SUCH AS SEEKING SUPPORT FROM TRUSTED FRIENDS OR SEEKING PROFESSIONAL HELP IF NEEDED.

PRAYER

DEAR GOD, THANK YOU FOR YOUR PROMISE TO BE WITH US AND STRENGTHEN US. HELP US TO TRUST IN YOUR FAITHFULNESS AND NOT GIVE IN TO FEAR AND ANXIETY. GUIDE US TO SEEK THE SUPPORT WE NEED AND TAKE PRACTICAL STEPS TO OVERCOME OUR FEARS. IN JESUS' NAME, AMEN.

Day 5: Living a Life of Integrity

"So that you may not be sluggish, but imitators of those who through faith and patience inherit the promises." - Hebrews 6:12

Do you feel like time is running out in terms of finding a partner or fulfilling your dreams? It's easy to become restless and impatient, but Hebrews 6:12 reminds us that faith and patience are key in inheriting the promises of God.

Just like Abraham who waited patiently for God to fulfill His promise of a son, we too must wait patiently for God's perfect timing. We can trust that God has a plan for our lives and that He will work everything out for our good (Romans 8:28).

Cultivating patience is not always easy,

BUT IT IS A FRUIT OF THE SPIRIT (GALATIANS 5:22-23) AND SOMETHING WE CAN ASK GOD TO HELP US WITH. WE CAN ALSO LOOK TO THE EXAMPLES OF THOSE WHO HAVE GONE BEFORE US AND IMITATE THEIR FAITH AND PATIENCE.

PRAYER

DEAR GOD, PLEASE HELP ME TO CULTIVATE PATIENCE IN MY LIFE. WHEN I AM FEELING RESTLESS OR ANXIOUS, HELP ME TO TRUST IN YOUR PERFECT TIMING AND HAVE FAITH THAT YOU HAVE A PLAN FOR MY LIFE. HELP ME TO IMITATE THE FAITH AND PATIENCE OF THOSE WHO HAVE GONE BEFORE ME AND TRUST THAT YOU WILL FULFILL YOUR PROMISES TO ME. AMEN.

Day 6: Learning to Love Yourself

"And the second [commandment] is like it: 'You shall love your neighbor as yourself.'" - Matthew 22:39

Getting caught up in the pressures of society and culture to achieve certain milestones by a certain age happens to the best of us. We can become so focused on achieving these goals that we forget to take care of ourselves in the process. However, Jesus teaches us that we are called to love our neighbor as ourselves.

This means that we must first love and take care of ourselves before we can effectively love and care for others. Learning to love yourself doesn't mean becoming selfish or self-centered, but rather acknowledging and accepting yourself just as you are and treating yourself with kindness and compassion.

ONE WAY TO START CULTIVATING SELF-LOVE IS BY TAKING CARE OF YOUR PHYSICAL HEALTH. THIS CAN MEAN GETTING REGULAR EXERCISE, EATING A BALANCED AND NUTRITIOUS DIET, GETTING ENOUGH SLEEP, AND TAKING TIME TO REST AND RELAX. IT'S ALSO IMPORTANT TO TAKE CARE OF YOUR MENTAL AND EMOTIONAL HEALTH BY PRACTICING SELF-CARE ACTIVITIES SUCH AS JOURNALING OR TALKING WITH A TRUSTED FRIEND OR THERAPIST. ADDITIONALLY, SETTING HEALTHY BOUNDARIES WITH OTHERS AND LEARNING TO SAY "NO" WHEN NECESSARY CAN ALSO BE AN ACT OF SELF-LOVE. WHEN YOU LEARN TO LOVE YOURSELF, YOU'LL FIND THAT IT BECOMES EASIER TO LOVE OTHERS AND BUILD MEANINGFUL RELATIONSHIPS.

PRAYER

DEAR GOD, PLEASE HELP ME TO SEE MYSELF AS YOU SEE ME - A BELOVED CHILD OF GOD. TEACH ME HOW TO LOVE AND TAKE CARE OF MYSELF SO THAT I CAN LOVE AND CARE FOR

OTHERS WELL. GIVE ME THE STRENGTH TO SET HEALTHY BOUNDARIES AND PRIORITIZE MY PHYSICAL, MENTAL, AND EMOTIONAL HEALTH. THANK YOU FOR YOUR CONSTANT LOVE AND CARE FOR ME. AMEN.

DAY 7: BUILDING HEALTHY RELATIONSHIPS

"A FRIEND LOVES AT ALL TIMES, AND A BROTHER IS BORN FOR A TIME OF ADVERSITY." - PROVERBS 17:17

NAVIGATING RELATIONSHIPS, WHETHER IT'S WITH FRIENDS, FAMILY, OR A POTENTIAL PARTNER, CAN BE CHALLENGING. HOWEVER, THE BIBLE REMINDS US THAT BUILDING HEALTHY RELATIONSHIPS IS ESSENTIAL FOR A FULFILLING LIFE. PROVERBS 17:17 EMPHASIZES THE IMPORTANCE OF HAVING FRIENDS WHO LOVE US THROUGH THICK AND THIN. TRUE FRIENDS ARE THERE FOR US NOT ONLY DURING THE GOOD TIMES BUT ALSO DURING THE TOUGH TIMES, OFFERING SUPPORT, ENCOURAGEMENT, AND LOVE.

TO BUILD HEALTHY RELATIONSHIPS, WE NEED TO BE INTENTIONAL ABOUT INVESTING TIME AND EFFORT IN THEM. IT INVOLVES BEING VULNERABLE, HONEST, AND TRANSPARENT WITH

OTHERS, PRACTICING ACTIVE LISTENING, FORGIVING, AND SEEKING RECONCILIATION WHEN CONFLICTS ARISE.

WE CAN ALSO LOOK TO JESUS AS AN EXAMPLE OF HOW TO BUILD HEALTHY RELATIONSHIPS. HE SHOWED COMPASSION, EMPATHY, AND KINDNESS TO EVERYONE HE ENCOUNTERED, AND HE ALWAYS PRIORITIZED PEOPLE ABOVE HIS OWN DESIRES AND NEEDS.

PRAYER

DEAR LORD, THANK YOU FOR THE GIFT OF RELATIONSHIPS. HELP US TO CULTIVATE HEALTHY RELATIONSHIPS IN OUR LIVES, STARTING WITH OUR RELATIONSHIPS WITH YOU. SHOW US HOW TO BE VULNERABLE, HONEST, AND TRANSPARENT WITH OTHERS, AND TEACH US HOW TO LOVE OTHERS AS YOU LOVE US. GUIDE US IN BUILDING STRONG FRIENDSHIPS AND FAMILY RELATIONSHIPS, AND HELP US TO BE A LIGHT IN THE LIVES OF THOSE AROUND US. AMEN.

Day 8: Pursuing God's Plan for Your Life

"For I know the plans I have for you," declares the Lord, "plans to prosper you and not to harm you, plans to give you hope and a future." - Jeremiah 29:11

At this age, it's common to question what the future holds and what God's plan for your life might be. It's easy to feel like you're running out of time or that you've missed your chance for certain things. But the truth is, God's plans for you are still unfolding, and they are good.

In Jeremiah 29:11, God promises that He has plans for you, plans that are good and hopeful. This doesn't mean that everything will be easy or that there won't be challenges, but it does mean that God has a purpose and a plan for your life that will ultimately lead to your prosperity and not your harm.

So how do you pursue God's plan for your life? First, seek Him through prayer and reading His Word. Ask Him to reveal His plan for you, and be open to His leading. Second, trust that He will guide you and provide for you every step of the way. And finally, be obedient to His leading, even if it means stepping out of your comfort zone or taking a risk.

Prayer

Dear God, thank You for Your promise that You have good plans for my life. Help me to trust in Your leading and guidance, and to be obedient to Your plan for me. Give me the courage to step out in faith, even when it's scary or uncomfortable. I trust in Your provision and guidance for my life. Amen.

Day 9: Letting Go of Control

"Trust in the Lord with all your heart and lean not on your own understanding; in all your ways submit to him, and he will make your paths straight." - Proverbs 3:5-6

Do you feel pressure to have your life together and under control? It's easy to fall into the trap of thinking that you need to have all the answers and be in charge of everything. But the truth is, we can never truly be in control of everything. Life is unpredictable, and sometimes things happen that are beyond our control. That's why it's important to learn to let go of control and trust in God.

Proverbs 3:5-6 reminds us to trust in the Lord with all our heart and not lean on our own understanding. God's ways are higher than our ways, and his plans for

OUR LIVES ARE PERFECT. WHEN WE TRY TO CONTROL EVERYTHING, WE LIMIT WHAT GOD CAN DO IN OUR LIVES. BUT WHEN WE TRUST IN HIM AND SUBMIT TO HIS WILL, HE CAN WORK IN US AND THROUGH US IN AMAZING WAYS.

LETTING GO OF CONTROL CAN BE SCARY, BUT IT'S ALSO FREEING. WHEN WE STOP TRYING TO CONTROL EVERYTHING, WE CAN EXPERIENCE PEACE AND JOY IN THE PRESENT MOMENT. WE CAN TRUST THAT GOD IS WORKING ALL THINGS TOGETHER FOR OUR GOOD AND HIS GLORY.

PRAYER

DEAR GOD, HELP ME TO LET GO OF CONTROL AND TRUST IN YOU. I KNOW THAT YOUR PLANS FOR MY LIFE ARE PERFECT, AND I WANT TO SUBMIT TO YOUR WILL. GIVE ME THE COURAGE TO TRUST YOU IN ALL AREAS OF MY LIFE, EVEN WHEN THINGS ARE UNCERTAIN. HELP ME TO EXPERIENCE YOUR PEACE AND JOY AS I LET GO OF CONTROL AND TRUST IN YOU. AMEN.

Day 10: Seeking God's Wisdom

"If any of you lacks wisdom, you should ask God, who gives generously to all without finding fault, and it will be given to you." - James 1:5

Every day we will face various challenges and decisions that require wisdom and discernment. Thankfully, we serve a God who generously gives us wisdom when we ask for it. However, we must come to God with a heart that is humble and open to receive His guidance.

It's important to remember that wisdom comes not only from knowledge and experience but also from the Holy Spirit. As we seek God's wisdom, we must also be willing to listen to His voice and obey His direction, even when it may not make sense to us.

When we lack clarity and direction in

OUR LIVES, WE CAN TURN TO GOD'S WORD FOR GUIDANCE. THE BIBLE IS FILLED WITH STORIES AND TEACHINGS THAT CAN HELP US GAIN PERSPECTIVE AND UNDERSTANDING. WE CAN ALSO SEEK COUNSEL FROM WISE AND MATURE BELIEVERS IN OUR LIVES WHO CAN OFFER GODLY WISDOM AND ADVICE.

PRAYER

DEAR GOD, I COME TO YOU TODAY ASKING FOR WISDOM AND DISCERNMENT. HELP ME TO TRUST IN YOUR GUIDANCE AND TO HAVE A HEART THAT IS OPEN TO RECEIVING YOUR DIRECTION. MAY I SEEK WISDOM FROM YOUR WORD AND FROM WISE BELIEVERS IN MY LIFE. HELP ME TO WALK IN OBEDIENCE TO YOUR WILL, EVEN WHEN IT MAY NOT MAKE SENSE TO ME. THANK YOU FOR YOUR PROMISE TO GIVE GENEROUSLY TO ALL WHO ASK FOR WISDOM. IN JESUS' NAME, AMEN.

Day 11: Seeking God's Wisdom

"You make known to me the path of life; in your presence, there is fullness of joy; at your right hand are pleasures forevermore." Psalm 16:11

It can be easy to get caught up in the pressure to achieve certain milestones or conform to societal expectations but this pressure can often rob us of the joy and fulfillment that comes from simply being present in the moment and finding contentment in the journey. Psalm 16:11 reminds us that true joy is found in God's presence and His plan for our lives.

When we learn to trust in God's timing and provision, we can experience the peace and joy that comes from knowing we are exactly where we are meant to be. Even in the midst of difficult circumstances or unmet expectations, we can hold onto the hope that God is working all things

TOGETHER FOR OUR GOOD.

So instead of constantly striving for the next thing or dwelling on what we don't have, let us learn to embrace the journey and find joy in each step along the way. Let us trust in God's plan and presence, knowing that He is with us and will lead us on the path of life.

Prayer

Heavenly Father, help me to find joy in the journey and trust in Your plan for my life. When I feel tempted to compare myself to others or focus on what I lack, remind me of Your presence and provision. Give me the strength and courage to embrace each day with gratitude and joy, knowing that You are with me every step of the way. In Jesus' name, Amen.

DAY 12: LIVING A LIFE OF GRATITUDE

"Give thanks in all circumstances; for this is God's will for you in Christ Jesus."
- 1 Thessalonians 5:18

It's easy to focus on the things we don't have or the things that haven't gone according to our plans. But as Christians, we are called to live a life of gratitude, even in the midst of difficult circumstances.

This means intentionally focusing on the good things in our lives and thanking God for them. It also means trusting that God is working all things together for our good, even when we can't see it.

One way to cultivate gratitude is to start a daily gratitude journal. Each day, write down at least three things you are thankful for. They can be big or small,

SIMPLE OR PROFOUND. THE ACT OF INTENTIONALLY LOOKING FOR THINGS TO BE THANKFUL FOR CAN HELP SHIFT OUR PERSPECTIVE AND MAKE US MORE AWARE OF GOD'S BLESSINGS IN OUR LIVES.

PRAYER

HEAVENLY FATHER, THANK YOU FOR ALL THE BLESSINGS YOU HAVE GIVEN ME, EVEN THE ONES I MAY TAKE FOR GRANTED. HELP ME TO CULTIVATE A HEART OF GRATITUDE AND TO TRUST THAT YOU ARE WORKING ALL THINGS TOGETHER FOR MY GOOD. AMEN.

Day 13: Serving Others with Love

"For you were called to freedom, brothers, and sisters; only do not use your freedom as an opportunity for self-indulgence, but through love become slaves to one another." - Galatians 5:13

As single women, it can be easy to focus on our own needs and desires. However, as followers of Christ, we are called to serve others with love. This means putting aside our own selfish desires and actively seeking ways to help and bless those around us.

One way to serve others is by volunteering at a local organization or charity. This could be a soup kitchen, a shelter, a community garden, or any other organization that serves those in need. By giving our time and resources, we can make a tangible difference in the

LIVES OF OTHERS AND SHOW THEM THE LOVE OF CHRIST.

ANOTHER WAY TO SERVE OTHERS IS BY INTENTIONALLY SEEKING OUT THOSE WHO MAY BE OVERLOOKED OR MARGINALIZED IN OUR COMMUNITIES. THIS COULD BE AN ELDERLY NEIGHBOR WHO LIVES ALONE, A SINGLE MOM WHO NEEDS HELP WITH CHILDCARE, OR SOMEONE WHO IS STRUGGLING WITH ADDICTION OR MENTAL HEALTH ISSUES. BY REACHING OUT TO THESE INDIVIDUALS AND OFFERING OUR SUPPORT AND ENCOURAGEMENT, WE CAN BE A LIGHT IN THEIR LIVES AND DEMONSTRATE THE LOVE AND COMPASSION OF CHRIST.

PRAYER

DEAR GOD, HELP US TO USE OUR FREEDOM TO SERVE OTHERS WITH LOVE. OPEN OUR EYES TO THE NEEDS OF THOSE AROUND US AND GIVE US THE COURAGE AND COMPASSION TO REACH OUT AND HELP. MAY OUR ACTIONS BE A REFLECTION OF YOUR LOVE AND GRACE, AND MAY WE BRING HOPE AND HEALING TO THOSE WHO ARE HURTING. AMEN.

Day 14: Forgiving Yourself and Others

"Be kind to one another, tenderhearted, forgiving one another, as God in Christ forgave you." - Ephesians 4:32

Forgiveness is a crucial part of living a healthy and fulfilling life. However, it can often be difficult to forgive others or even ourselves. Yet, the Bible teaches us that we should forgive others just as God has forgiven us through Christ.

Holding onto grudges and bitterness can lead to emotional pain and even physical ailments. Forgiveness frees us from the burden of anger and resentment, allowing us to move forward with love and compassion.

Perhaps you have been hurt by someone in the past and find it difficult to let go

OF THAT PAIN. OR MAYBE YOU HAVE MADE MISTAKES IN YOUR OWN LIFE AND STRUGGLE TO FORGIVE YOURSELF. WHATEVER THE CASE MAY BE, KNOW THAT GOD'S GRACE IS SUFFICIENT AND HE IS ALWAYS WILLING TO FORGIVE US. ASK GOD TO HELP YOU RELEASE ANY UNFORGIVENESS IN YOUR HEART AND REPLACE IT WITH HIS LOVE AND COMPASSION.

PRAYER

DEAR GOD, I ASK FOR YOUR HELP IN FORGIVING THOSE WHO HAVE HURT ME AND ALSO IN FORGIVING MYSELF FOR MY OWN MISTAKES. PLEASE HELP ME TO RELEASE ANY ANGER, BITTERNESS, OR RESENTMENT IN MY HEART AND REPLACE IT WITH YOUR LOVE AND COMPASSION. THANK YOU FOR YOUR ENDLESS GRACE AND FORGIVENESS. IN JESUS' NAME, AMEN.

Day 15: Practicing Self-Care

"Do you not know that your bodies are temples of the Holy Spirit, who is in you, whom you have received from God? You are not your own; you were bought at a price. Therefore honor God with your bodies." - 1 Corinthians 6:19-20

No matter your age, it's important to take care of yourself both physically and emotionally. You are a temple of the Holy Spirit, and it's important to honor God by taking care of your body. This means getting enough sleep, eating a healthy diet, exercising regularly, and taking time for self-care activities that help you relax and recharge.

It's also important to take care of yourself emotionally. Make time for activities that bring you joy and fulfillment, such as hobbies or spending time with loved ones.

Practice self-compassion and forgiveness, and don't be too hard on yourself when things don't go as planned.

Prayer

Dear God, please help me to take care of myself both physically and emotionally. Guide me in making healthy choices for my body and help me to find joy and fulfillment in my daily life. Thank you for your love and grace. Amen.

Day 16: Staying Focused on God's Promises

"For no matter how many promises God has made, they are 'Yes' in Christ. And so through him, the 'Amen' is spoken by us to the glory of God." - 2 Corinthians 1:20

It's easy to get discouraged when things don't go according to plan or when it feels like God's promises are taking too long to come to fruition. But this verse reminds us that God's promises are always fulfilled and that they are all "Yes" in Christ. This means that every promise in the Bible is available to us through our relationship with Jesus.

When we stay focused on God's promises, we can find comfort, hope, and strength in even the most difficult circumstances. We can trust that God is working all things together for our

GOOD (ROMANS 8:28) AND THAT HIS PLANS FOR US ARE GOOD (JEREMIAH 29:11).

SO LET US STAY FOCUSED ON GOD'S PROMISES AND TRUST THAT HE WILL FULFILL THEM IN HIS PERFECT TIMING. LET US CLING TO HIS WORD AND FIND PEACE IN THE MIDST OF UNCERTAINTY.

PRAYER

DEAR GOD, HELP US TO STAY FOCUSED ON YOUR PROMISES AND TO TRUST IN YOUR TIMING. GIVE US THE STRENGTH AND FAITH TO BELIEVE THAT YOU ARE WORKING ALL THINGS TOGETHER FOR OUR GOOD. HELP US TO FIND PEACE AND COMFORT IN YOUR WORD, EVEN IN THE MIDST OF DIFFICULT CIRCUMSTANCES. THANK YOU FOR YOUR UNFAILING LOVE AND FAITHFULNESS. AMEN.

Day 17: Taking Risks in Faith

"Now faith is confidence in what we hope for and assurance about what we do not see." - Hebrews 11:1

It's often tempting to stick to what is safe and comfortable in our lives, but God often calls us to step out in faith and take risks. This requires confidence in the hope we have in God's promises and assurance that He will guide and protect us.

The heroes of faith listed in Hebrews 11 all had one thing in common: they stepped out in faith, often without knowing how their situations would turn out. Abraham left his home to follow God's call, not knowing where he was going. Moses trusted God to deliver the Israelites from slavery, even when Pharaoh refused to let them go. By faith, these men and women persevered through trials and

OVERCAME OBSTACLES.

WE TOO CAN STEP OUT IN FAITH, TRUSTING IN GOD'S PROMISES AND GUIDANCE. IT MAY NOT ALWAYS BE EASY OR COMFORTABLE, BUT THE REWARDS CAN BE GREAT. AS WE TAKE RISKS IN FAITH, WE OPEN OURSELVES UP TO NEW EXPERIENCES AND OPPORTUNITIES TO GROW AND SERVE OTHERS. LET US HAVE CONFIDENCE IN THE HOPE WE HAVE IN GOD AND STEP OUT IN FAITH TO FOLLOW HIS LEADING.

PRAYER

HEAVENLY FATHER, THANK YOU FOR THE HOPE WE HAVE IN YOU AND THE PROMISES YOU HAVE GIVEN US. HELP US TO HAVE CONFIDENCE IN YOUR GUIDANCE AND PROTECTION AS WE STEP OUT IN FAITH TO TAKE RISKS FOR YOUR KINGDOM. GIVE US THE COURAGE AND STRENGTH TO PERSEVERE THROUGH ANY TRIALS OR OBSTACLES WE MAY FACE. MAY OUR FAITH INSPIRE OTHERS TO TRUST IN YOU AS WELL. IN JESUS' NAME, AMEN.

Day 18: Building a Strong Foundation

"Therefore everyone who hears these words of mine and puts them into practice is like a wise man who built his house on the rock. The rain came down, the streams rose, and the winds blew and beat against that house; yet it did not fall, because it had its foundation on the rock. But everyone who hears these words of mine and does not put them into practice is like a foolish man who built his house on sand. The rain came down, the streams rose, and the winds blew and beat against that house, and it fell with a great crash." - Matthew 7:24-27 (NIV)

Building a strong foundation is essential in every aspect of life. Just like a house, our lives need to be built on a solid foundation in order to withstand the storms of life. In this passage, Jesus teaches about two builders, one who built his house on a rock and the other who built his house on sand. The house built on the rock withstood the storms, while

THE HOUSE BUILT ON SAND COLLAPSED.

As women in our 30s, it's important to have a strong foundation in our faith, our values, and our sense of self-worth. We need to build our lives on the rock-solid foundation of God's word, which provides us with guidance, wisdom, and direction. When we build our lives on this foundation, we can trust that no matter what storms come our way, we will remain standing.

However, if we build our lives on a foundation of sand, such as worldly values, material possessions, or the opinions of others, we will find ourselves collapsing under the weight of life's challenges. It's easy to get caught up in the fleeting pleasures of this world, but they will never bring the lasting peace and security that we crave.

So let us take time to examine the foundation of our lives. Are we building

ON A SOLID FOUNDATION OF FAITH IN GOD, OR ARE WE BUILDING ON SAND? LET US CHOOSE TO BUILD OUR LIVES ON THE ROCK OF GOD'S WORD, SO THAT WE MAY STAND FIRM IN THE FACE OF ANY STORM THAT COMES OUR WAY.

PRAYER

HEAVENLY FATHER, HELP US TO BUILD OUR LIVES ON A STRONG FOUNDATION OF FAITH IN YOU. GIVE US THE WISDOM TO DISCERN WHAT IS TRULY IMPORTANT IN LIFE, AND THE COURAGE TO BUILD OUR LIVES ACCORDINGLY. MAY WE TRUST IN YOUR WORD AND FIND SECURITY IN YOUR PROMISES, KNOWING THAT YOU ARE ALWAYS WITH US, EVEN IN THE MIDST OF LIFE'S STORMS. AMEN.

Day 19: Using Your Gifts and Talents

"Each of you should use whatever gift you have received to serve others, as faithful stewards of God's grace in its various forms." - 1 Peter 4:10

It can be easy to feel like you are not living up to your full potential. Maybe you're not where you thought you would be in your career or you haven't found a way to use your talents to serve others. It can be tempting to compare yourself to others and feel like you're not measuring up.

But the truth is, God has given you unique gifts and talents that are meant to be used for His purposes. As 1 Peter 4:10 reminds us, each of us has received a gift that we are called to use to serve others. Whether it's a talent for music, a passion for writing, or a heart for

HOSPITALITY, THERE IS A WAY THAT YOU CAN USE YOUR GIFTS TO MAKE A DIFFERENCE IN THE LIVES OF THOSE AROUND YOU.

THE KEY IS TO BE FAITHFUL STEWARDS OF THE GRACE THAT GOD HAS GIVEN US. WE ARE NOT CALLED TO USE OUR GIFTS FOR OUR OWN GLORY OR TO IMPRESS OTHERS, BUT TO USE THEM IN SERVICE TO GOD AND HIS KINGDOM. WHEN WE USE OUR GIFTS IN THIS WAY, WE CAN EXPERIENCE A SENSE OF PURPOSE AND FULFILLMENT THAT COMES FROM KNOWING THAT WE ARE MAKING A DIFFERENCE IN THE WORLD.

PRAYER

DEAR GOD, THANK YOU FOR THE GIFTS AND TALENTS THAT YOU HAVE GIVEN ME. HELP ME TO USE THEM IN SERVICE TO OTHERS AND TO BE FAITHFUL STEWARDS OF YOUR GRACE. SHOW ME HOW I CAN MAKE A DIFFERENCE IN THE WORLD AND GIVE ME THE COURAGE TO STEP OUT IN FAITH AND USE MY GIFTS FOR YOUR PURPOSES. AMEN.

Day 20: Finding Peace in God's Presence

"Be still, and know that I am God; I will be exalted among the nations, I will be exalted in the earth." - Psalm 46:10

In today's fast-paced world, it can be easy to get caught up in the hustle and bustle of everyday life. We are constantly bombarded with messages telling us to do more, be more, and achieve more. It can feel overwhelming, and it's easy to lose sight of what truly matters. That's why it's so important to take time to be still and connect with God.

Psalm 46:10 reminds us to "be still, and know that I am God." When we take the time to be still and quiet our minds, we create space for God to speak to us. It's in those moments of stillness that we can feel God's presence and hear His voice. It's where we can find peace in the midst

OF CHAOS.

So how do we practice stillness in a world that never stops moving? It starts with intentionally carving out time in our day for quiet reflection. This might mean waking up a few minutes earlier in the morning to sit in silence and pray, or taking a walk in nature during our lunch break. Whatever form it takes, the important thing is to make stillness a priority in our lives.

Prayer

Dear God, help me to be still and connect with you today. In the midst of the chaos of life, help me to create space for your presence and to hear your voice. Thank you for the peace that comes from knowing you. Amen.

Day 21: Moving Forward in Faith

"Brothers and sisters, I do not consider myself yet to have taken hold of it. But one thing I do: Forgetting what is behind and straining toward what is ahead, I press on toward the goal to win the prize for which God has called me heavenward in Christ Jesus." - Philippians 3:13-14

As we come to the end of this devotional, we are reminded to press on toward the goal that God has set for us. We may have faced challenges, setbacks, and even failures along the way, but we are encouraged to forget what is behind us and strive toward what is ahead.

The Apostle Paul, in his letter to the Philippians, expressed his own determination to move forward in faith. Despite his past as a persecutor of

CHRISTIANS AND HIS CURRENT CIRCUMSTANCES AS A PRISONER, HE REMAINED FOCUSED ON CHRIST AND THE ETERNAL PRIZE THAT AWAITED HIM. HE WROTE, "I PRESS ON TOWARDS THE GOAL TO WIN THE PRIZE FOR WHICH GOD HAS CALLED ME HEAVENWARD IN CHRIST JESUS." (PHILIPPIANS 3:14)

SIMILARLY, WE TOO ARE CALLED TO KEEP OUR EYES FIXED ON JESUS AND THE ETERNAL REWARDS THAT AWAIT US. WE ARE NOT TO BE HELD BACK BY OUR PAST MISTAKES OR CURRENT STRUGGLES, BUT TO PRESS ON IN FAITH AND CONTINUE TO SEEK GOD'S WILL FOR OUR LIVES.

AS WE MOVE FORWARD IN FAITH, WE CAN BE CONFIDENT THAT GOD IS WITH US EVERY STEP OF THE WAY. HE HAS PROMISED TO NEVER LEAVE US OR FORSAKE US (HEBREWS 13:5), AND HIS GRACE IS SUFFICIENT FOR US IN ALL THINGS (2 CORINTHIANS 12:9).

LET US, THEREFORE, NOT BE DISCOURAGED BY THE CHALLENGES AND OBSTACLES WE MAY FACE, BUT RATHER BE INSPIRED TO PRESS ON IN FAITH,

TRUSTING IN THE ONE WHO HAS CALLED US AND
EQUIPPED US TO DO HIS WILL.

PRAYER

HEAVENLY FATHER, WE THANK YOU FOR THE
FAITH AND PERSEVERANCE OF THE APOSTLE
PAUL AND FOR THE EXAMPLE HE SET FOR US IN
PRESSING ON TOWARD THE GOAL. HELP US TO
FORGET WHAT IS BEHIND US AND TO STRIVE
TOWARDS WHAT IS AHEAD, WITH OUR EYES FIXED
FIRMLY ON JESUS. STRENGTHEN US TO FACE THE
CHALLENGES AND OBSTACLES THAT MAY COME
OUR WAY, AND REMIND US THAT YOUR GRACE IS
SUFFICIENT FOR US. MAY WE CONTINUE TO SEEK
YOUR WILL FOR OUR LIVES AND TRUST IN YOUR
GUIDANCE AND PROVISION. IN JESUS' NAME,
AMEN.

CONCLUSION

As we come to the end of this devotional, we hope that it has been a source of encouragement, inspiration, and growth in your journey with God. These 21 devotionals have covered a wide range of topics, from trusting in God's timing to practicing self-care and forgiveness. Our prayer is that these daily reflections have helped you to deepen your faith and develop a closer relationship with God.

In your 30s, life can feel like a balancing act. You may be juggling career goals, family responsibilities, and personal aspirations, all while trying to navigate the ups and downs of relationships and friendships. It can be easy to lose sight of what's truly important in the midst of all the noise. That's why taking time each day to pause and reflect on God's Word is so crucial.

Our hope is that these devotionals have helped you to see yourself through God's eyes - as a beloved daughter, worthy of love and respect. We hope that they have reminded you of God's goodness and faithfulness, even in the midst of challenging circumstances. And we pray that they have encouraged you to keep moving forward in faith, trusting that God has a plan and purpose for your life.

We encourage you to continue seeking God's guidance and wisdom as you journey through your 30s and beyond. And remember, you are not alone. God is with you every step of the way, and there is a community of believers who are cheering you on. We hope that this devotional has been a helpful resource for you, and we pray that it will continue to bless you for years to come.